Traceable Faces for Cloth Dolls

By Barb Spencer

Publisher

Gregory Bayer

Editor

Kim Shields

Production Team

Cindy Boutwell

Cindy McCarville

Jean Adams

Jones Publishing, Incorporated

N7450 Aanstad Road

P.O. Box 5000

Iola, WI 54945

Phone: (715) 445-5000

Fax: (715) 445-4053

Traceable Faces for
Cloth Dolls

By Barb Spencer

Published By:

Jones Publishing, Incorporated

N7450 Aanstad Road

P.O. Box 5000

Iola, WI 54945 U.S.A.

Phone: (715) 445-5000

Fax: (715) 445-4053

This book is available at special quantity discounts for bulk purchases. For prices or other information, contact Greg Bayer at the above address.

10 9 8 7 6 5 4 3 2 1

Printed in the United States

ISBN 1-879825-16-3 $9.95

About the Author

Barb Spencer is one of America's leading cloth doll designers. She is especially known for her wonderful doll faces. Barb has designed dolls for many publishers, fabric and lace companies, as well as for doll collectors. Her original designs and doll models have been represented in international markets, showcased in national advertising and used in cloth dollmaking class presentations and demonstrations. Barb's one-of-a-kind dolls have been displayed in museums, galleries, expo centers, doll festivals and quilt markets.

Also, she has had another of her books on doll faces used in art classes. *The Enchanted Attic: Impressions with Expressions* was Barb's first book on doll faces. It included over 80 faces for cloth doll ladies, animals, Santas, and clowns. She also writes "Hints From the Attic," a regular column for *Dollmaking* magazine. The column features problem-solving tips for cloth dollmakers.

In addition to her published writing, Barb owns a store which specializes in original dolls and patterns for cloth dolls. Needless to say, her life is filled with her "little friends."

Please Read This!

This book was produced for the entertainment and enlightenment of cloth dollmakers. While every effort has been made to ensure that the information contained herein is correct and up-to-date, the editor, author, and publisher extend no warranty as to the accuracy or completeness of the information—there may be mistakes, both typographical and in content. Therefore, this text should be used only as a general guide and not as the ultimate source of information.

This book is sold with the understanding that the publisher is not engaged in rendering product endorsements or providing instruction as a substitute for appropriate training by qualified sources. Therefore, Jones Publishing, Inc. and the author, Barb Spencer, shall have neither liability nor responsibility to any person or entity with respect to any loss or damage caused, or alleged to be caused, directly or indirectly, by the information contained in this book.

We hope that you enjoy reading *Traceable Faces for Cloth Dolls*.

Table of Contents

Introduction

Few things about a doll are as moving as its face. Looking at a just-completed doll is like looking at a newly-born family member. How many of us finish creating a doll and say "Look at that adorable little face!"? We're fascinated by the detail of the eyes, nose, and mouth — their regularities or irregularities. As artists, we enjoy integrating these features correctly and proportionally into the basic oval shape of a face. Or, we may want to personalize a doll by varying the shape of its faces, making it a little more square, long, narrow, or round than any other.

Dolls should evoke happiness. After all, we all need friendly faces in our lives. There are many styles of faces, each of which may touch a special place in our hearts. For example, a whimsical face may give rise to laughter, while a nostalgic "period" face evokes memories of bygone times. The effective design of a doll's face can bring that character's personality to life, bringing joy to you and others for many generations to come. What an exciting legacy to pass on to children, family members, and friends!

Recently, I attended a doll show where my main interest was cloth dolls. But tucked in-between some beautiful porcelain and clay dolls was a chalk doll that I had to bring home to sit on the shelf directly in front of my computer screen, just a little above eye level. I knew this was the little face I wanted before me while I composed this book. Hands tucked under her chin, with a pondering look on her face, Winny is very inspirational. Of course, the other doll friends I've created and collected over the years are motivating as well, and they mean a lot to me, which is why I decided to share their adorable little faces with you via this book.

As you might imagine, my house is full of dolls, a few of which are from my childhood. Regretfully, very few of my childhood dolls survived my younger sister. Luckily, though, my favorite doll did survive (barely). This doll, named Shirley, is a lady who stands 14 inches tall. When she got a little worse for wear, my mother would take her to the "doll hospital" for repairs and a new wardrobe. Shirley had everything from specialty hats to every kind of footwear imaginable. I've had her missing arms and bedraggled wig replaced, and legs restrung. I also made her a new outfit and bought her new shoes and socks. Ah, little sisters! I fussed over her night and day for many years. Little did I know what an impact Shirley would have on my life. I think it is because of her that I especially love designing narrow-bodied, 12- to 18-inch dolls with pretty faces. Looking back, I know it was my mother who made my love for dolls possible. Every Christmas she took me to one of our local department stores where I could choose any doll from a beautiful selection. My face gets flushed just recalling the excitement!

Whether I'm creating a doll for competition, a customer, or myself, I always design the face first. If I have a special look to design, I begin by searching through my home library of doll-related books, which includes notebooks full of clippings taken from doll magazines, for an idea. If this does not work, I go to one or several libraries. Sometimes my doll faces are modeled after someone I saw in a store, or an actress I saw on television or in the movies. The research is fun, and the sketching even more fun. I'm confident this book will become a valuable part of your dollmaking library, as the instructions and traceable faces will assist you in creating beautiful doll faces. ✂

Selecting Fabric for Your Doll's Face

You have several choices of fabric to select from for your doll faces. My favorite is a high quality of unbleached muslin. It is ideal for tinting or dyeing, and accepts the application of various media without the stretching, raveling, or snagging problems sometimes encountered with other fabrics. However, you may prefer using bleached muslin.

Osnaburg is a nice fabric if you are making a country/folk doll. Its weave is looser than muslin, so zigzagging edges is a given. Since the fabric has more give, beware of stretching when stuffing your doll face. I have only used osnaburg as is, or tea dyed. It is more difficult to apply various media to osnaburg for facial features, except embroidery. Even then you should be careful not to pull threads too tightly.

Cotton linen has the appearance of a tighter woven osnaburg with linen, so it lends itself well to smaller dolls. Like osnaburg, its weave is looser than muslin, so zigzagging edges is also required. I have only used cotton linen as is—never tinted or dyed. It has the same characteristics as osnaburg. Flesh—colored cotton is also nice for doll faces. Linen is a good fabric to use for doll faces. It should be treated as osnaburg and cotton linen.

Knits are used mainly when needle sculpting. When using knit, take care to prevent runs in your fabric.

A cream—colored challis may be used, also. However, it is difficult to work with. I have never tinted or dyed challis. It frays very easily, so it needs to be zigzagged around the edges. It also easily runs like knit and nylon.

A cream or pale pink shade of satin may be used to create doll faces as well. It too is difficult to work with. Since it frays badly, it needs to be zigzagged around the edges. It runs if you aren't very careful. Generally, I have used satin for dolls without features.

Preparation of Fabric

All types of fabric should be washed before using, then tumble or hand dry. If the fabric is wrinkled, run an iron over it.

To achieve a flesh tone on one yard of unbleached muslin, I recommend tinting it with "Rit" brand dye. I like the result of adding a small amount (i.e., 1/8 teaspoon or less) of rose pink Rit Dye to 3 to 4 quarts of boiling water in a large soup stock pan (which you no longer use for cooking). If this is not enough color for your liking, add a little more dye. You may enhance the soft pinkish flesh tone by adding 1/8 teaspoon (or less) of tangerine dye. Again, if this is not enough color for your liking, add a little more dye. If you are not happy with the appearance of your tinted muslin, start all over by washing the dye out of the fabric with "Clorox" brand bleach in your washing machine water. After bleaching, wash your fabric in regular laundry detergent.

For an aged look, tea—dye your fabric, or use tan Rit Dye. For tea dying one yard of unbleached muslin, place 15 tea bags into 3 to 4 quarts of boiling water, and steep for 10 minutes. Using a long-handled wooden spoon, move the unbleached muslin around in the tea mixture to insure that a uniform color is achieved. If this is the color you like, remove your fabric and squeeze out as much moisture as possible. If the fabric is not as dark as you like, return the fabric to your tea mixture for another 10 minutes. When you have your desired color, squeeze the fabric dry and place it in the dryer to set the dye.

To seal the surface of your fabric for the application of facial features, spray it with aerosol hair spray and then let it air dry, or use a hair dryer. To dry — air dry, or use a hair dryer.

Selection of Tools & Supplies

Some of the basic tools and supplies that you will possibly need for tracing and completing your doll face, cutting the fabric, and sewing the head, include the following: Light box (or light table), #2 lead pencil, fabric eraser, basic sewing needle, a 5 1/8" or 7" dollmaking needle, sewing machine, tracing paper, vinyl plastic sheets for templates, template marking pencil, 8" dressmaker shears, preemie scissors, straight pins, cotton/polyester blend and quilting thread, permanent-ink fine-tip fabric pens, acrylic paints, watercolors, crayons, embroidery floss, embroidery floss color card, colored pencils, powered blush, powered eye shadow, stuffing tool, round wooden toothpicks, #00 paint brush, empty permanent-ink fine-tip fabric pen or empty ball point pen, cotton swabs, aerosol hair spray, blow dryer, and polyester filling.

Selecting the Size & Shape of Doll Heads

First, decide what age you want your doll to represent. Most dolls are made to represent a baby, toddler, child or adult. Since most formulas for the size of a doll begin with multiplying the head size, you have the advantage.

Remember that a real baby, birth through one year old, is approximately four heads tall (see illustration #1). A toddler, two through four years old, is approximately four and one-half heads tall. A child, five through ten years old, is approximately six and one-half heads tall. An adult is approximately seven and one-half to eight heads tall. This is a good formula for figuring doll sizes.

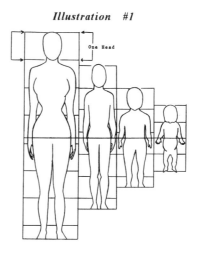

Illustration #1

One Head

Remember, too, that children — proportionally — have a larger head than body. Doll heads are sometimes even larger because they are not usually meant to be totally realistic. A head for any age doll may be exaggerated or understated to express a certain feeling or idea.

(One-fourth inch seam allowances should be added to all traceable faces in this book, except for the ones with broken lines on the inside of the solid outer line. These have already had the seam allowance added.)

The shapes of your doll heads will vary, depending on the look you wish to achieve and your taste. The most simple head, as far as I am concerned, is the attached flat head (see illustration #2). This means that the doll's head, neck and torso are in one piece. The head itself may be a basic oval shape but you may make it one that is more narrow, fat, round, square, or long.

In my opinion, the next most simple head is one that is cut into a basic oval, and not attached to the neck (see illustration #3A). This head may be sewn or glued (preferably sewn) to the neck tab on the doll torso (see illustration #3B), or the neck tab inserted into the head (see illustrations #3C) and then sewn (see illustration #3D).

Illustration #2

  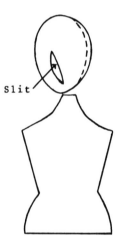 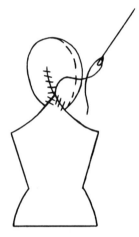

Illustration #3A   *Illustration #3B*   *Illustration #3C*   *Illustration #3D*

To make a head with a seamed nose, cut a regular outer shape with an inner opening at the top. This opening is for the nose and the seam allowance. The back of the head may have a dart at the top, or be left solid. (See illustration #4.) There are other methods of shaping a doll head. These include a center seamed face

Illustration #4

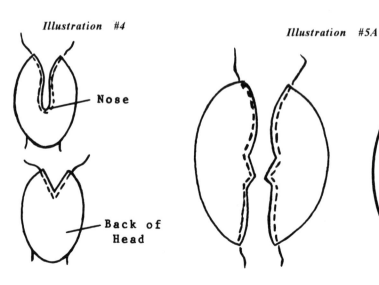

Nose

Back of Head

Illustration #5A

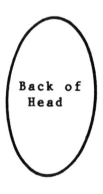

Back of Head

with a non-seamed back of the head (see illustration #5A) and a rounded head consisting of a front, two sides and a back (see illustration #5B).

Illustration #5B

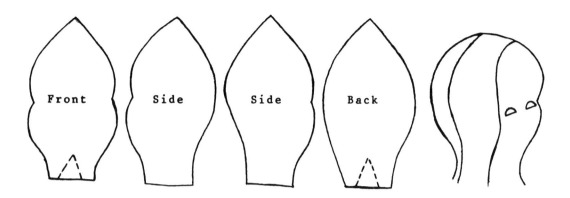

Cutting & Reinforcing the Doll Head

After drawing the doll head or head/body combination, trace that onto a template. (Templates are invaluable for making a good pattern. I use vinyl plastic sheets that are advertised for use with quilt patterns and templates). A template pencil should be used to trace your pattern piece(s) onto the vinyl plastic sheet. The marks will be visible for cutting purposes, after which they can be removed easily with a damp tissue or cloth. Cut out your template pattern, trace around its edge onto the fabric of your choice, and then cut out your doll head from fabric of choice. I recommend sewing a small zigzag stitch around the dol! head for reinforcement. If this isn't done, and you stuff the head firmly, the fabric may fray.

Tracing Doll Faces

Spray the "right" side (the surface that will be seen on the outside of a finished doll) of your doll fabric with aerosol hair spray. Let it dry naturally, or use a blow dryer. Place the "wrong" side of an existing drawn face onto your light box (or light table), then place the wrong side of your doll head fabric on top of this. Using a #2 lead pencil, lightly trace all of the facial features onto the right side of your cloth. If you need to erase something, use a fabric eraser. Trace over pencil markings with a brown permanent-ink fine-tip fabric pen.

Note: If you do not have a light box, or light table, use a window with direct sunlight, a glass coffee table with a light shining up from beneath, or white bond paper under the face you are tracing.

Finishing the Face

My color preferences for finishing the face are: brown, black, blue, red, and pink. Permanent-ink fine-tip fabric pens work well for the brows, eyes, nose, and lips. For the lips, choose a shade of acrylic paint, that compliments the doll's clothing (i.e., pink, peach, or red). Use white acrylic paint for highlighting the eyes. Select shades of pink or peach powdered blush for the cheeks, and colored pencils or powdered eye shadow for the eyelids.

Eyebrows: When the eyebrows don't need to be filled with color, I either leave the brown tracing lines to serve as the eyebrows, or I enhance the eyebrows by lightly coloring underneath them with black ink from a fabric pen. If the doll's hair is black, I cover the brown tracing lines for the eyebrows with a black ink fabric pen. If the eyebrows need to be filled with color, do so with feathering lines. (See illustration #6.)

Eyes: Lightly shade the iris with a blue or brown fabric pen. Firmly shade the pupil with a black fabric pen. Lightly apply black spoke lines to the eye, from the edge of the pupil to the outside of the iris. Using a fabric pen, firmly apply black ink to three sides of the eye — on the top and the two sides (this gives the eyes definition). Using the point of a wooden toothpick, or the point of an empty pen,

Illustration #6

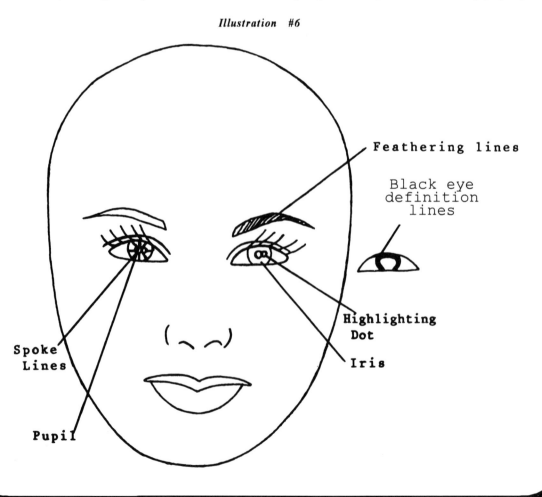

Feathering lines

Black eye definition lines

Highlighting Dot

Iris

Spoke Lines

Pupil

firmly apply a small amount of white acrylic paint to the left or right side of doll's pupil. Place highlighting dots in the same position on each eye — both dots to the left, or to the right. (See illustration #6.)

Nose: The brown tracing lines are sufficient.

Mouth: Fill in the brown tracing lines with pink, peach, or red using shades of permanent-ink or acrylic paints. If using the acrylic paints, apply with a wooden toothpick, or the point of an empty pen.

Drawing Doll Faces

Using the basic oval-shaped face, divide it in half vertically and horizontally to create four equal segments to the face (see illustration #7).

Locate the eyes on the center horizontal line. There should be one entire eye length between the doll's two eyes. The distance from the outer edge of each eye to each side of the face should equal the length of one eye. Faces should be five eyes wide, but this rule may be broken. (However, any given "rule" may be broken.)

Opened normally, the eye's width is half of its own length. The eyebrows are located about one-half a eye's length above the eyes.

The rule is that the inside corners of the doll's eyes should line up with the outside edges of the nose, or the bottom width of the nose equals the length of one eye. But, sometimes I make the nose narrower, especially on a very small doll face.

Draw a vertical line down from the center of each eye. Place the mouth within these two vertical lines. Divide the distance between the nose and chin into thirds, and place the mouth about 1/3 of the way down. Or place the mouth approximately half an eye's length under the nose. The width of the top lip is usually about 1/3 the depth of the mouth. The bottom of the lower lip about is halfway between the bottom of the nose and the chin length or one eye's length below the nose. ✄

Illustration #7

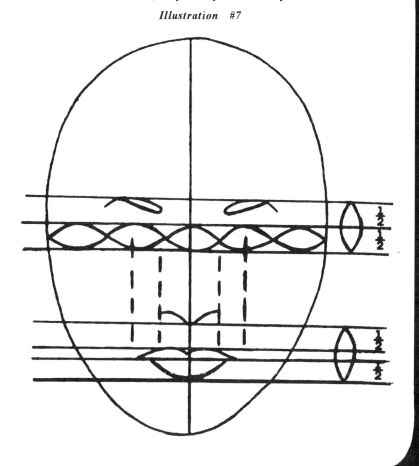

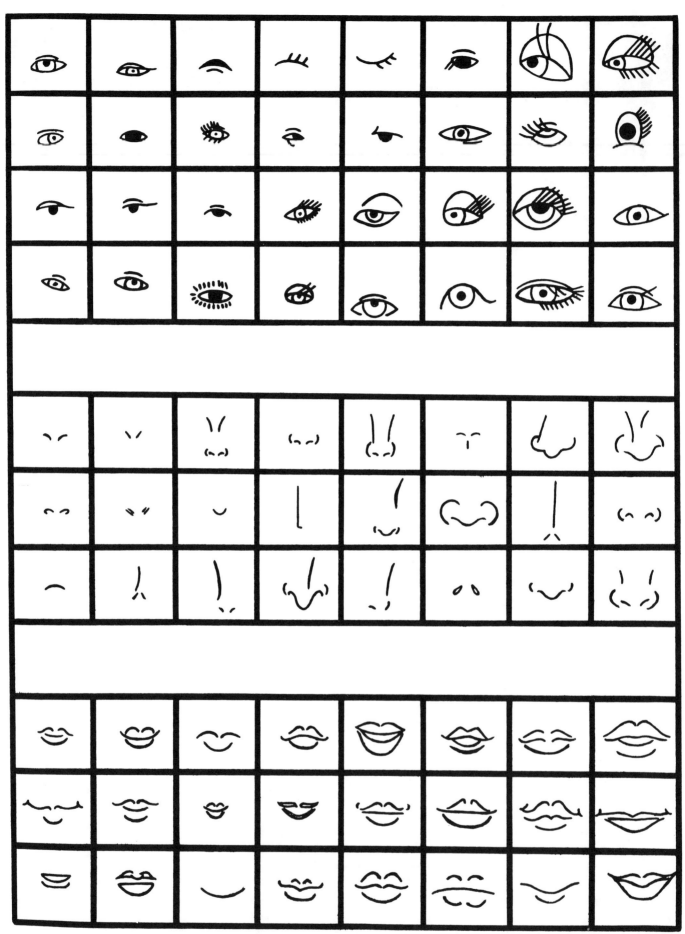

Facial features that dollmakers may use to design their own doll faces.

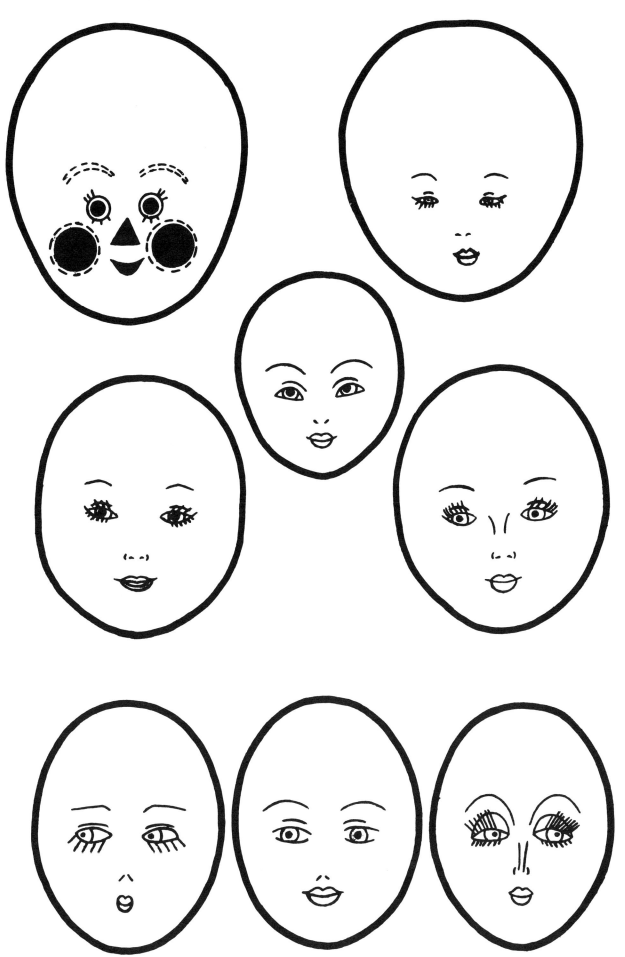

Traceable Faces for Cloth Dolls

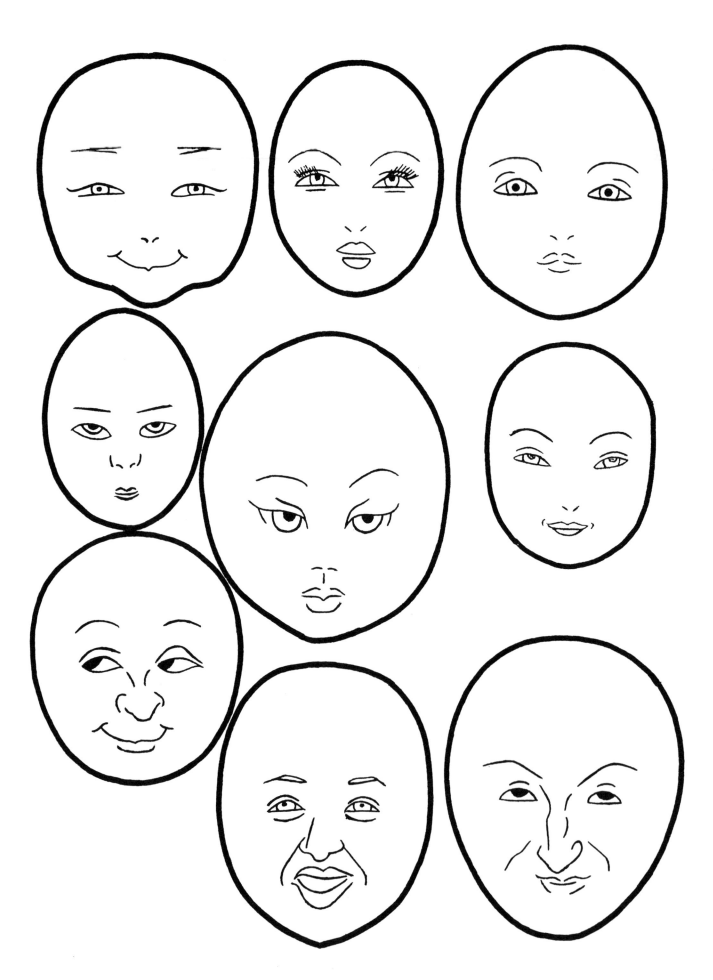

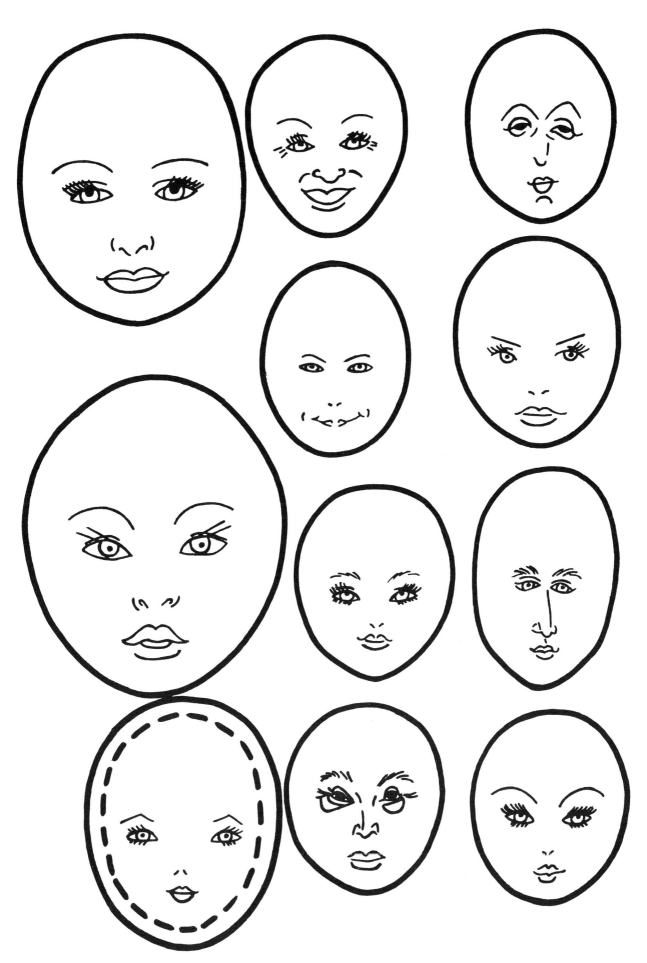

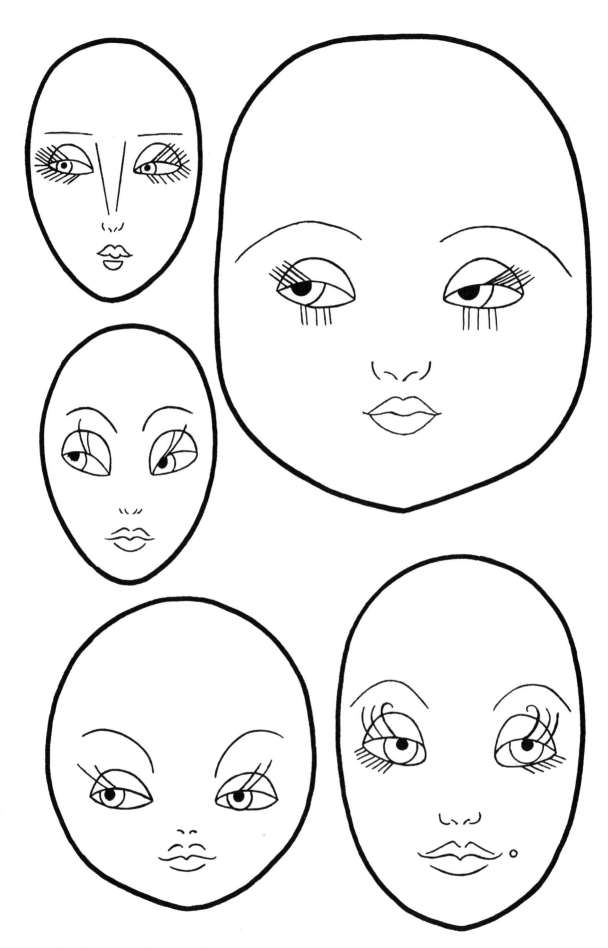

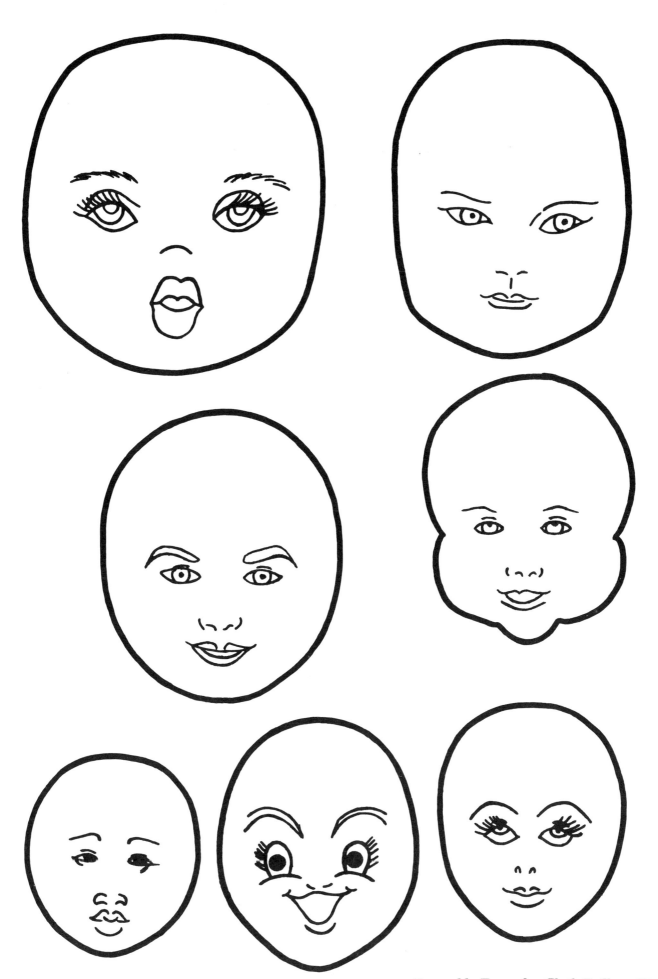

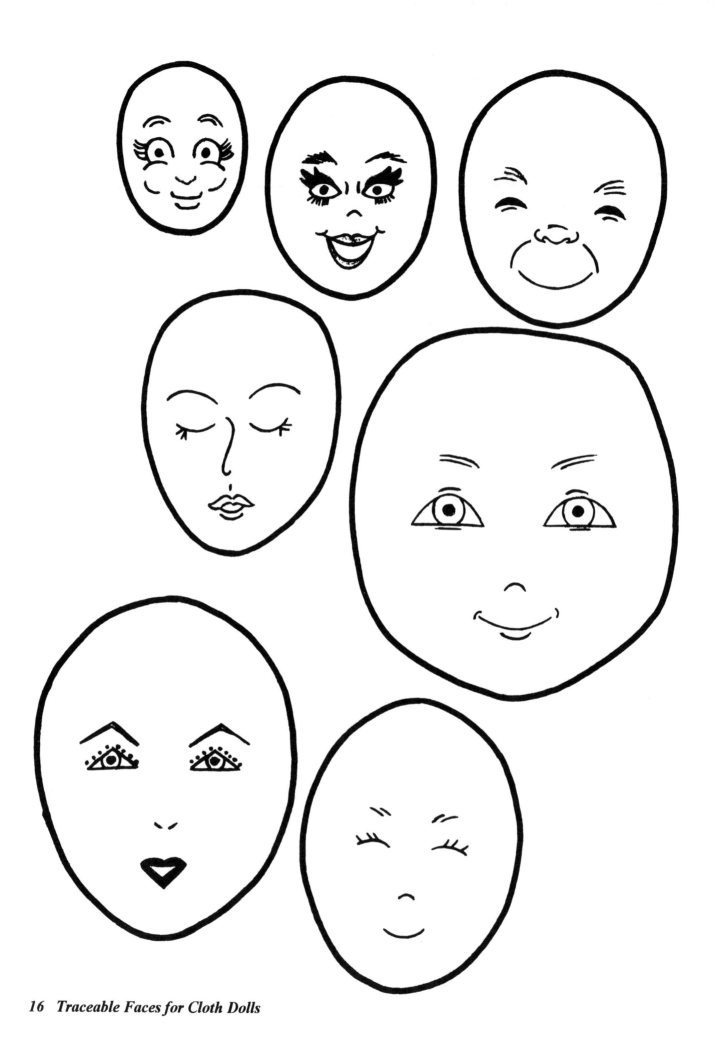

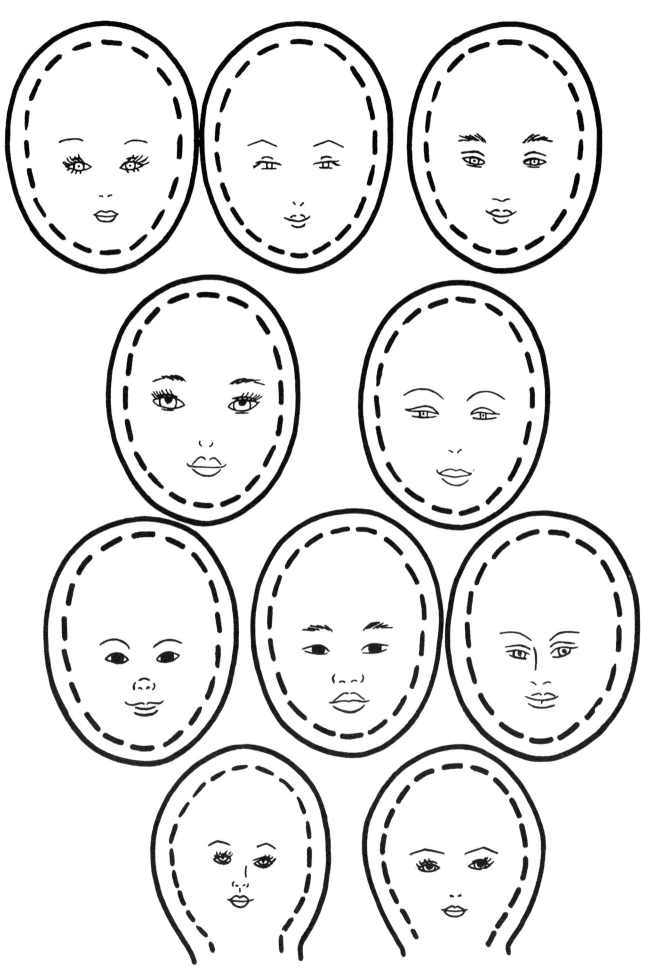

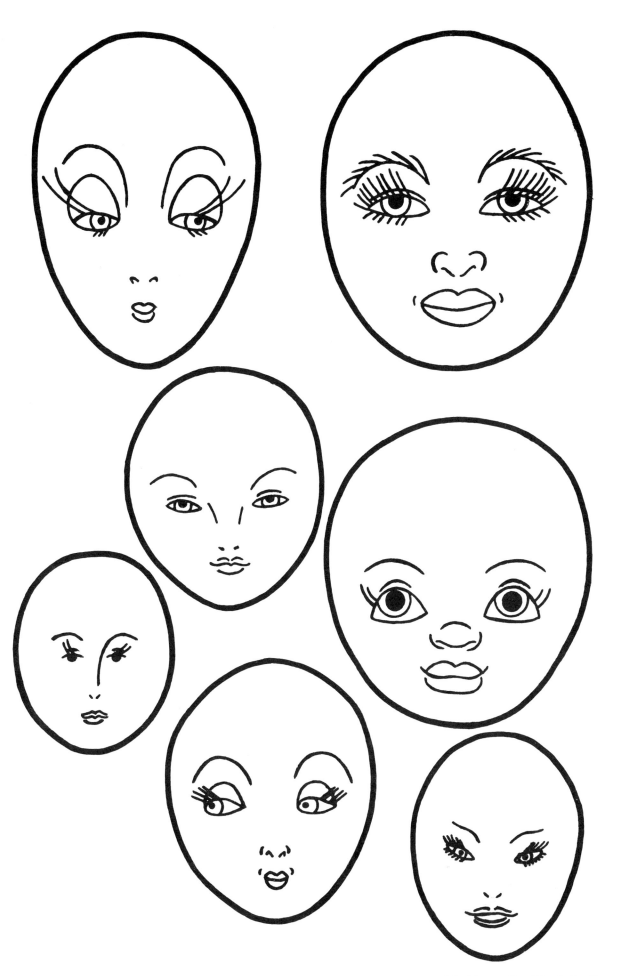

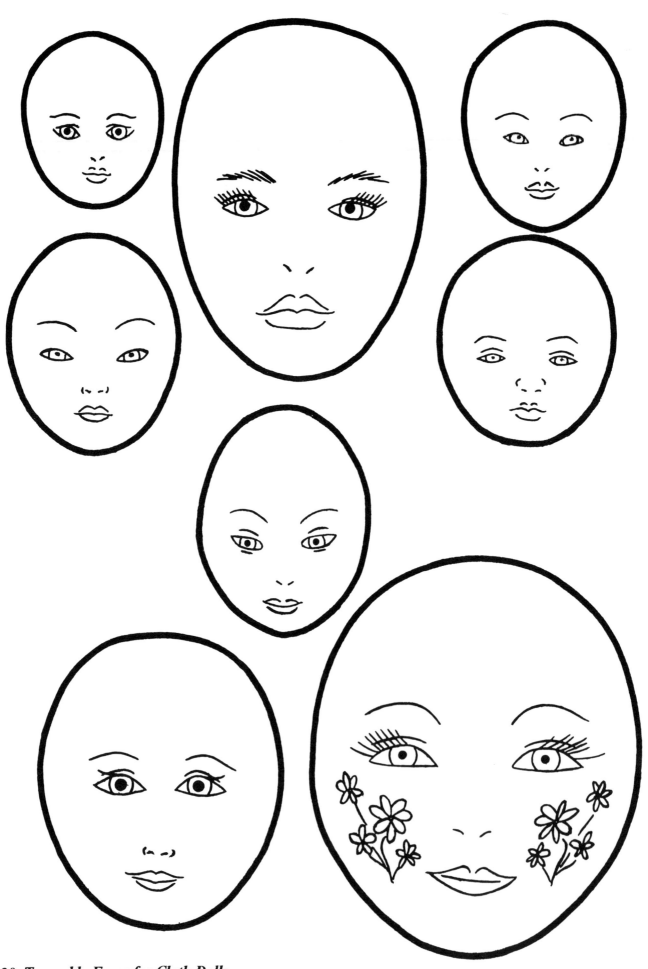

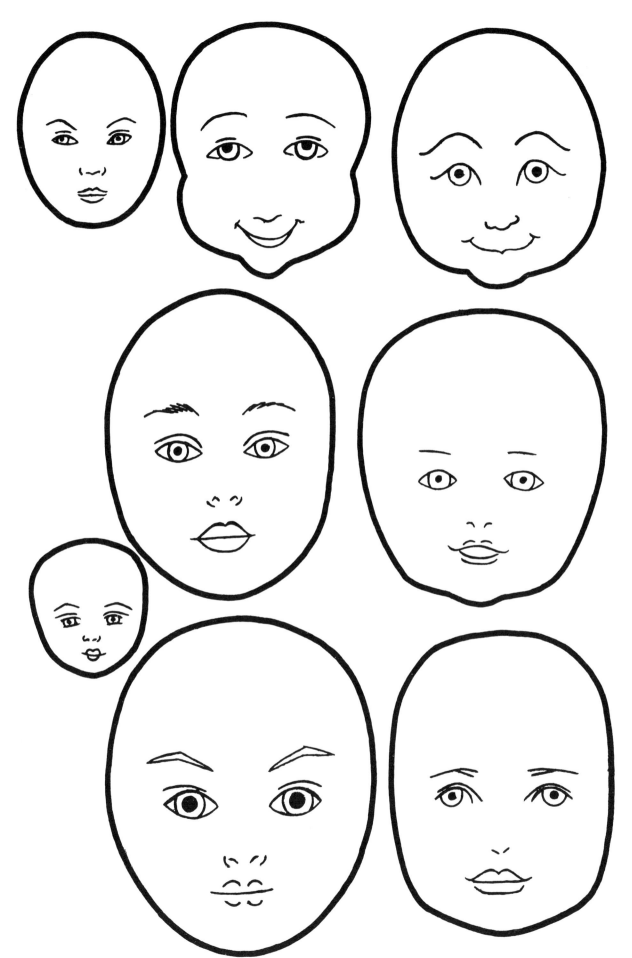

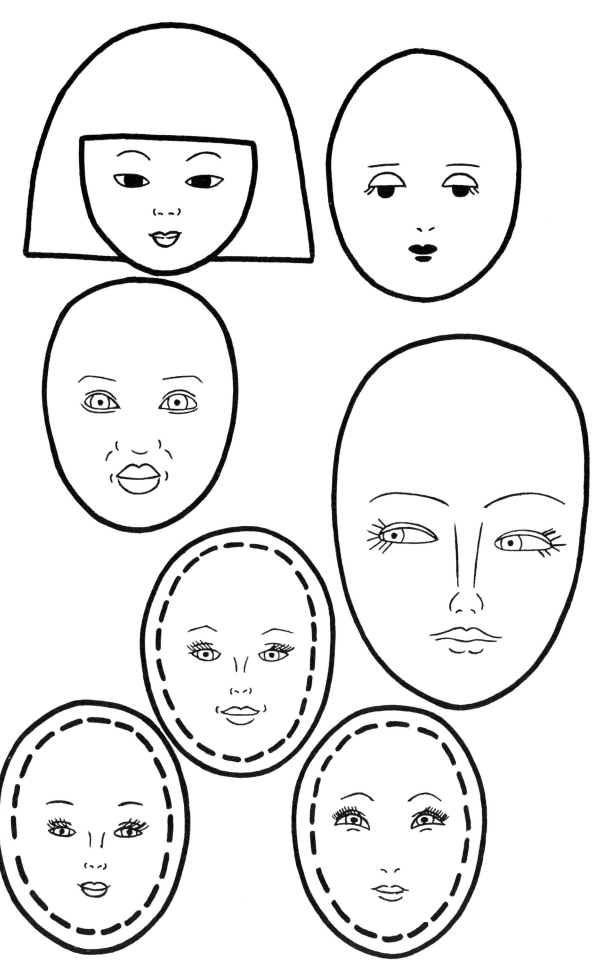

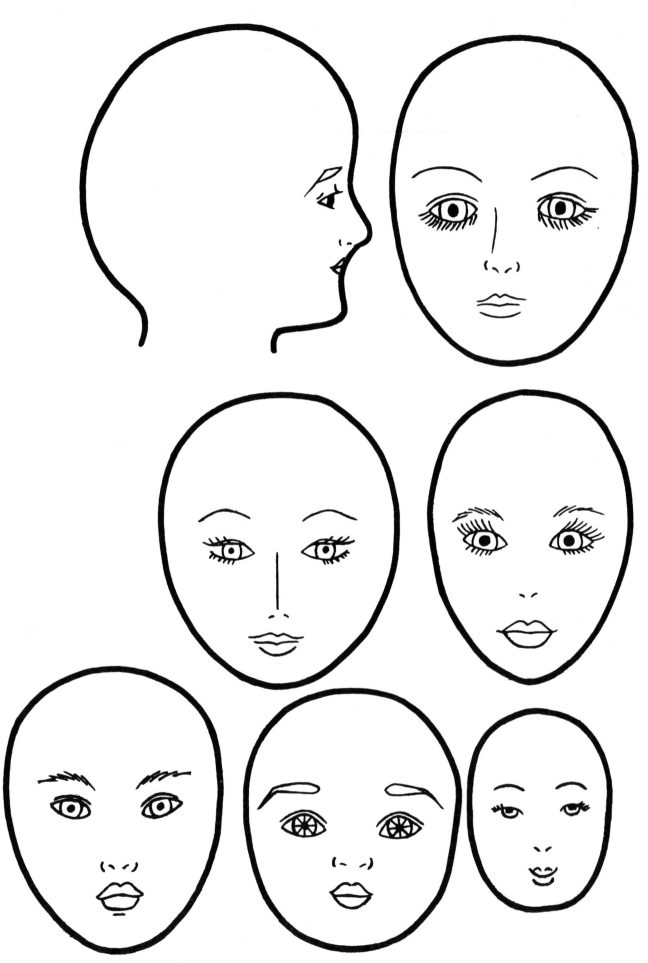

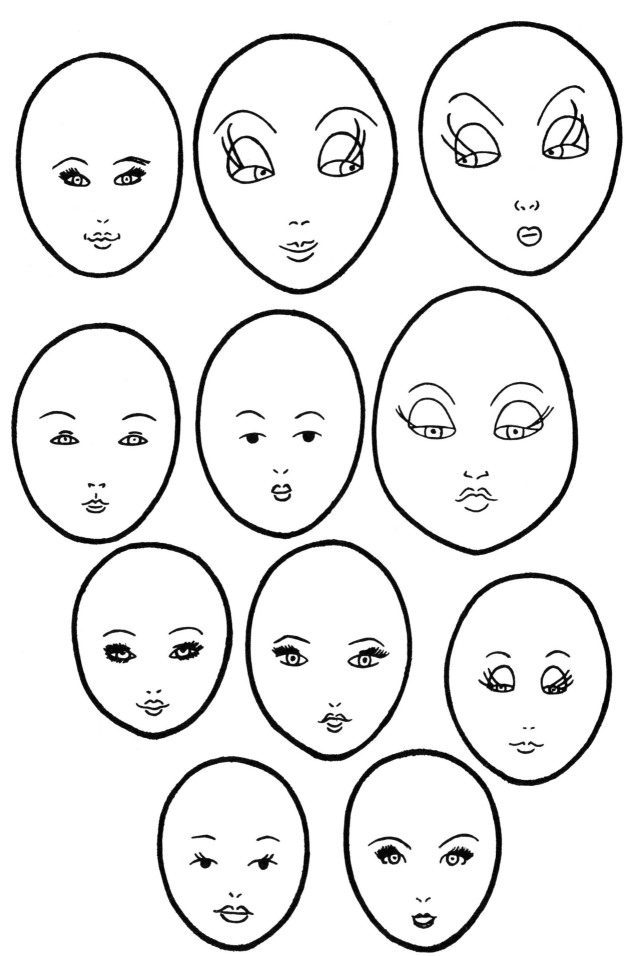

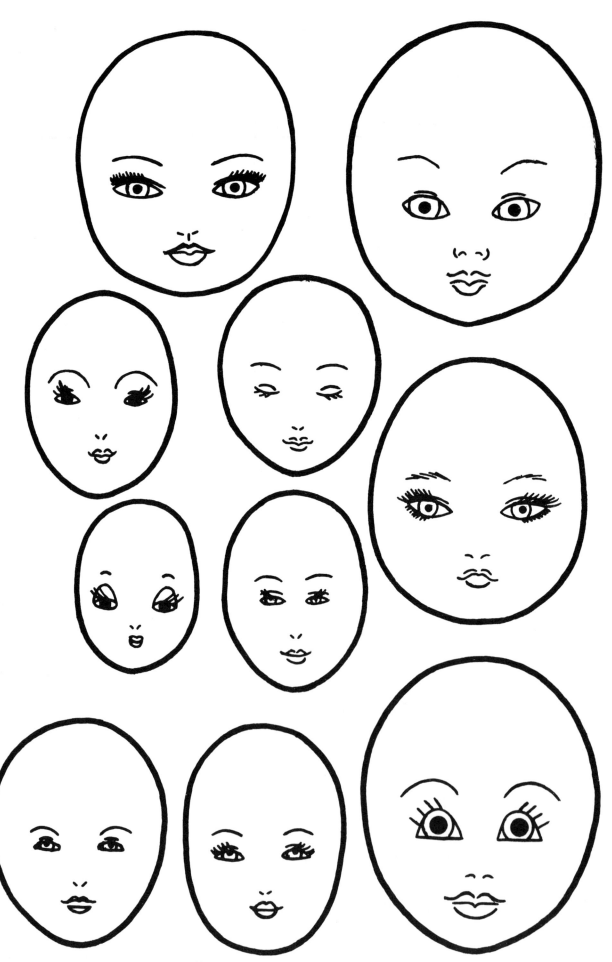

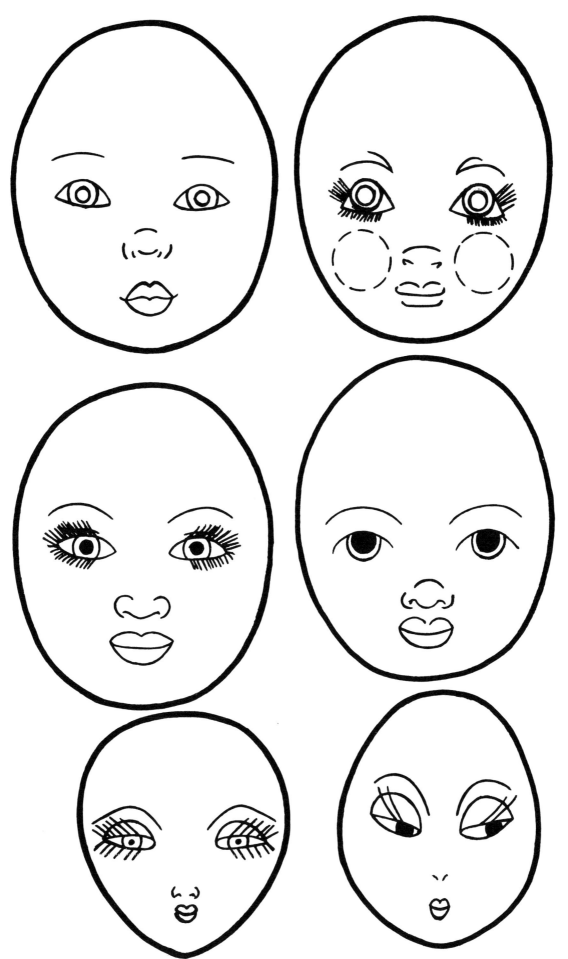

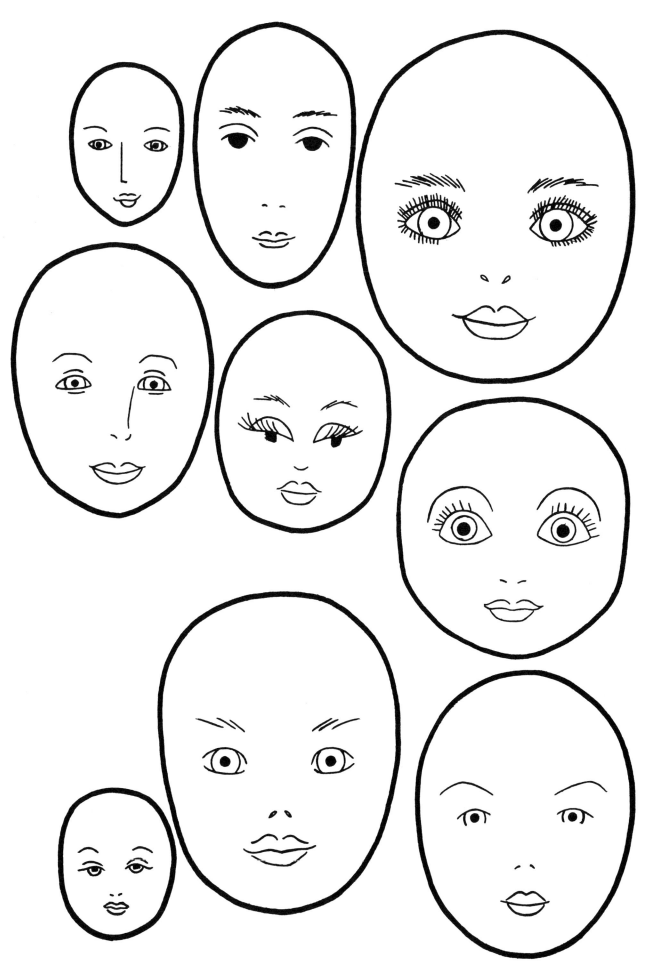

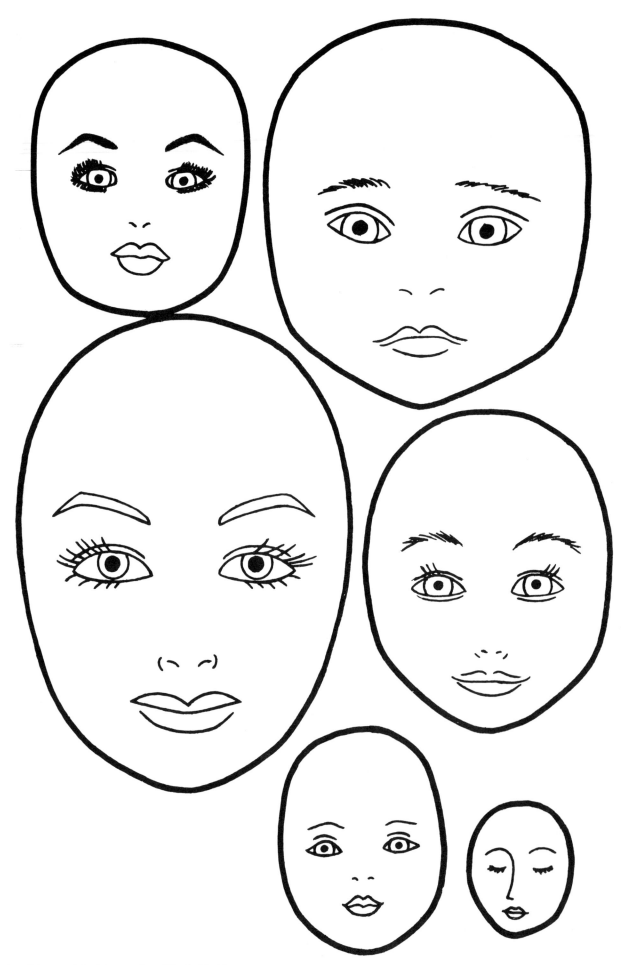

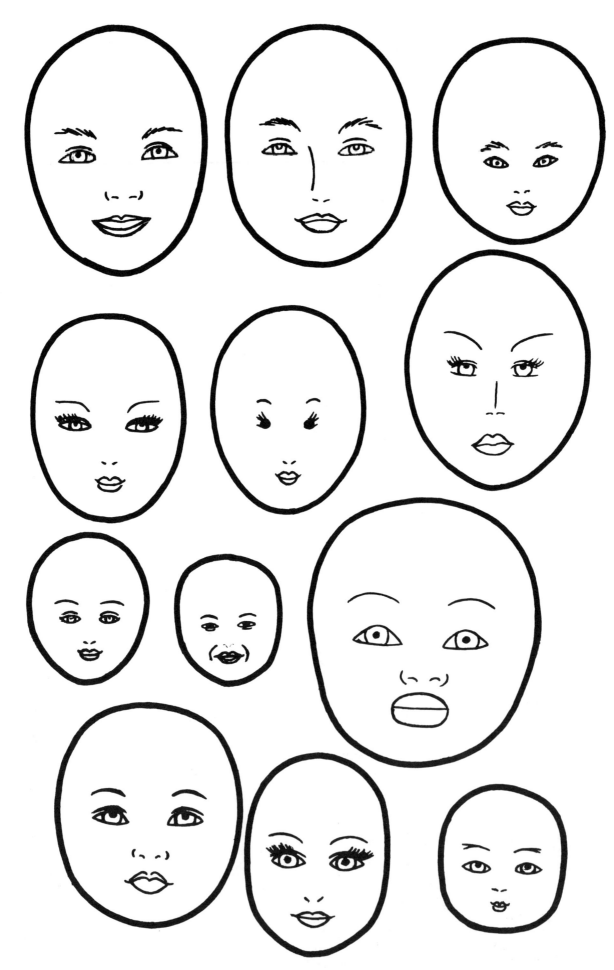

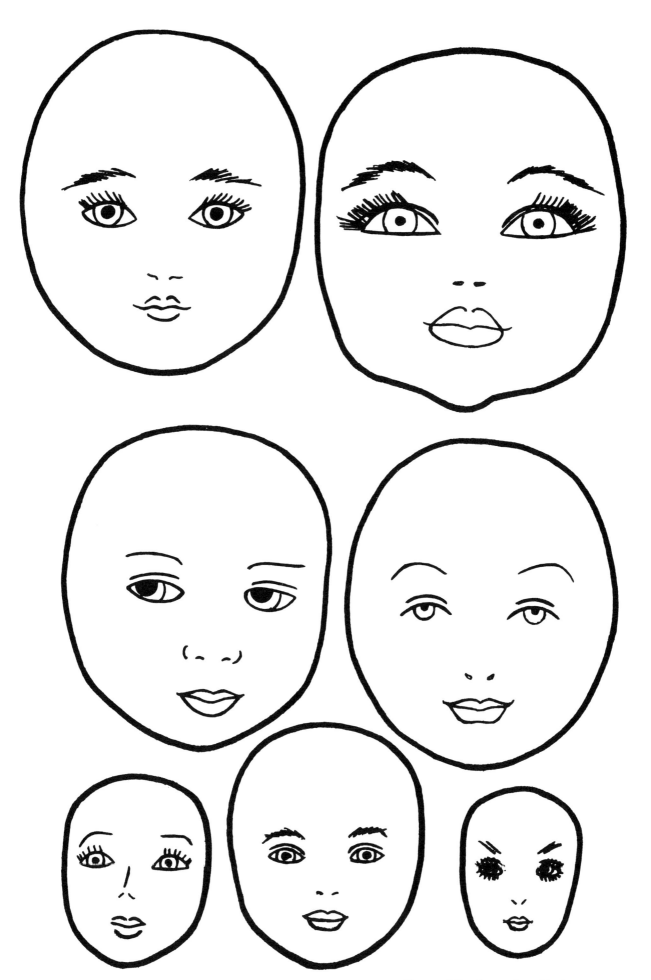

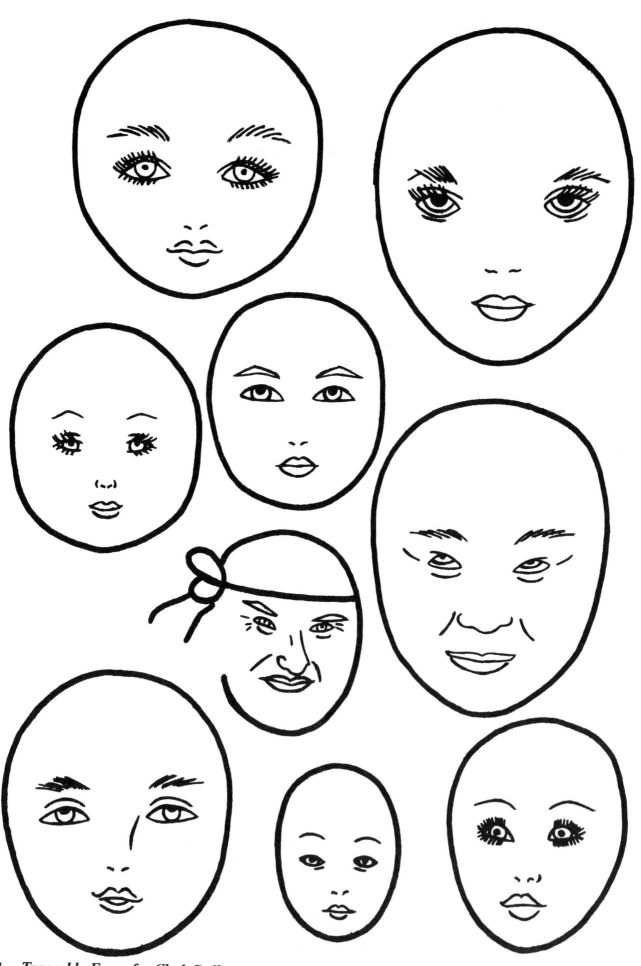

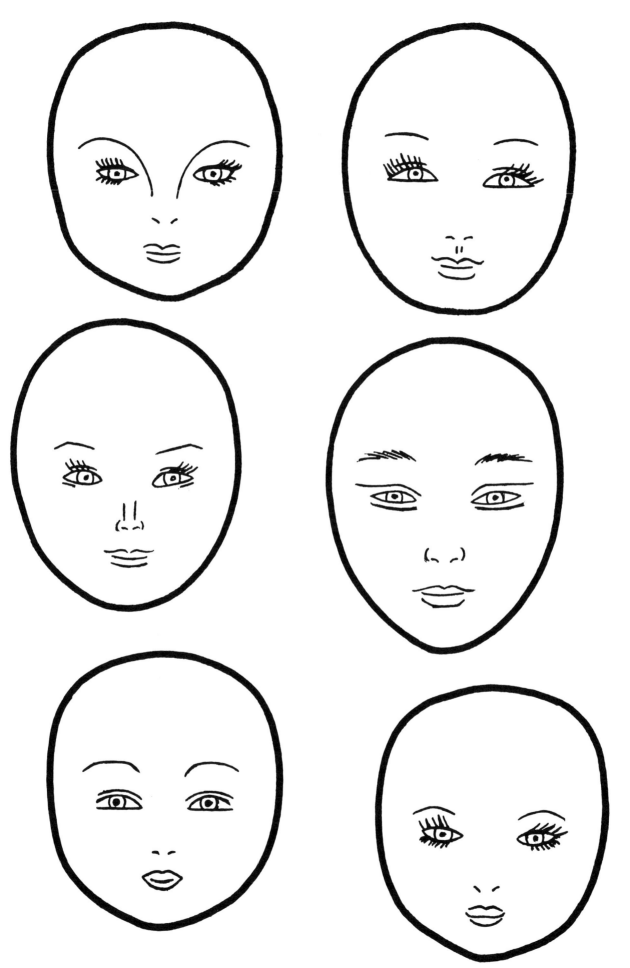

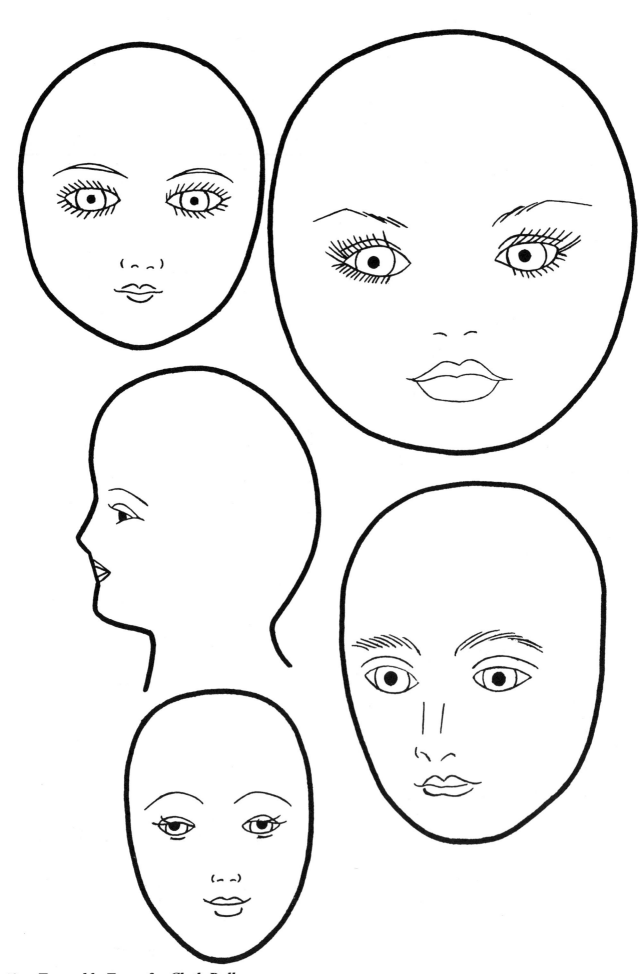

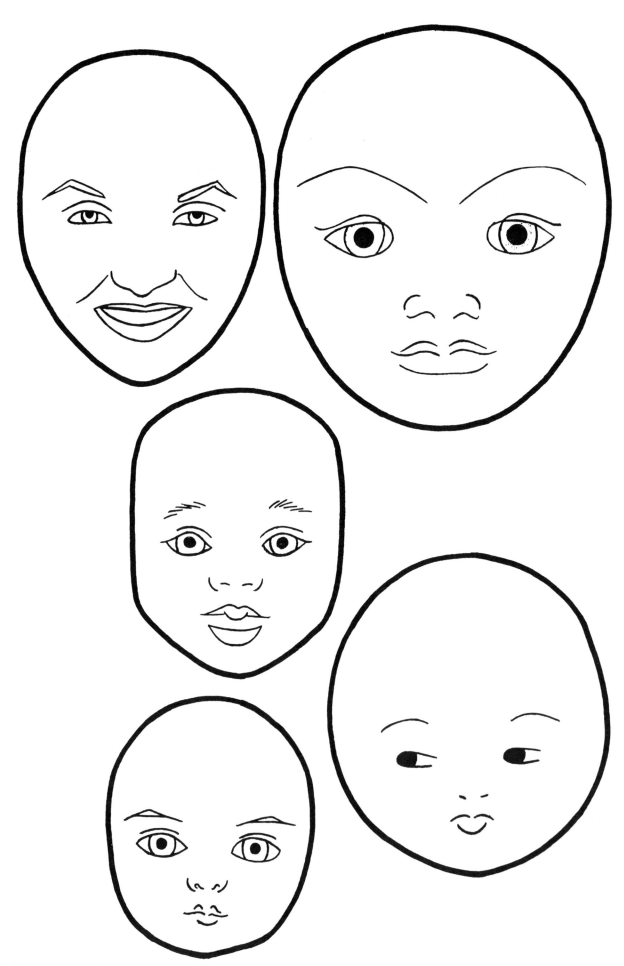

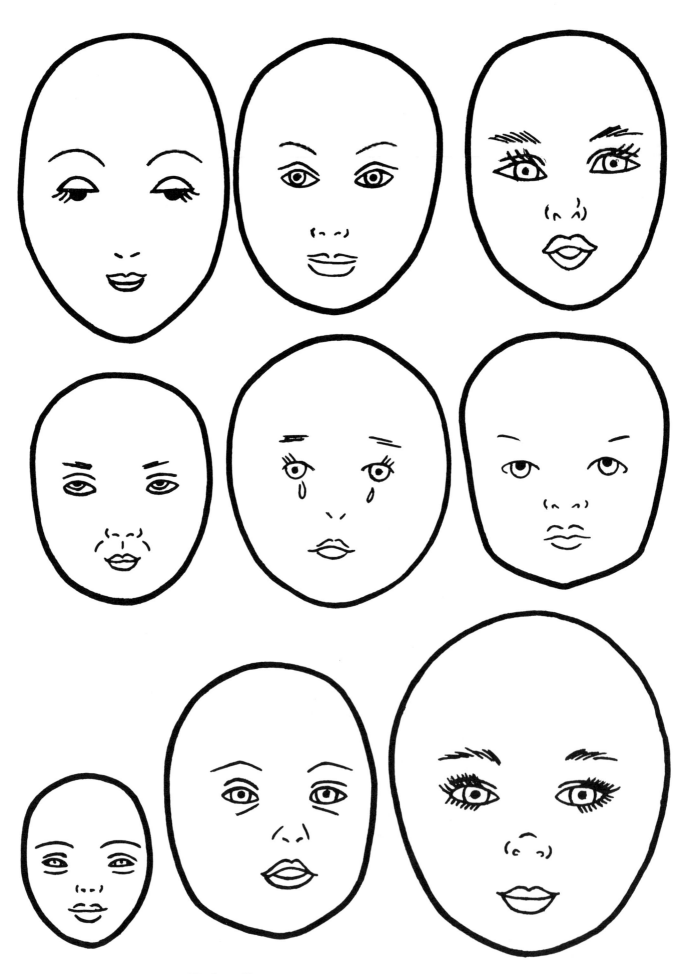

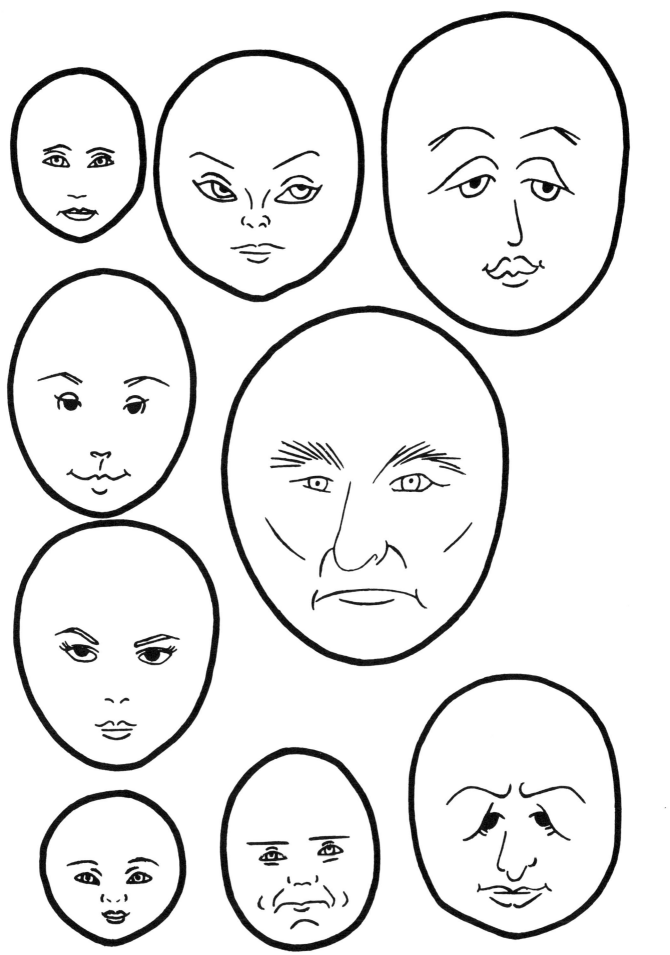

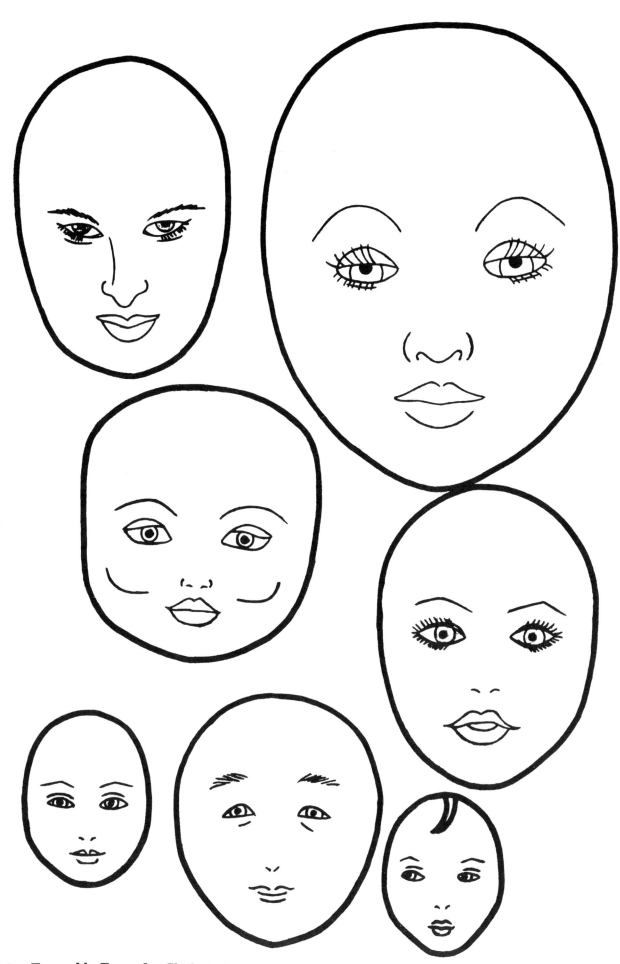

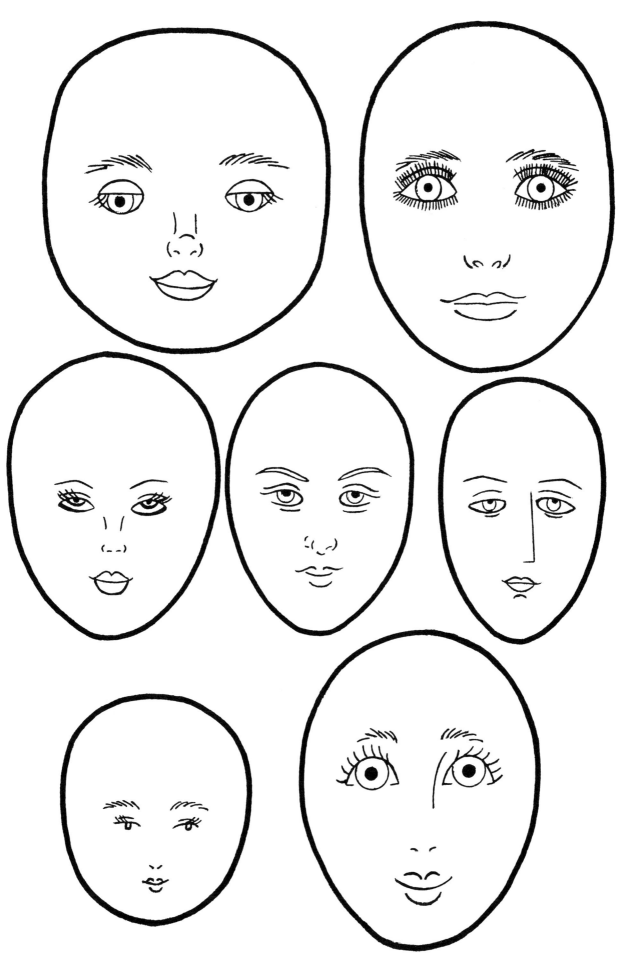

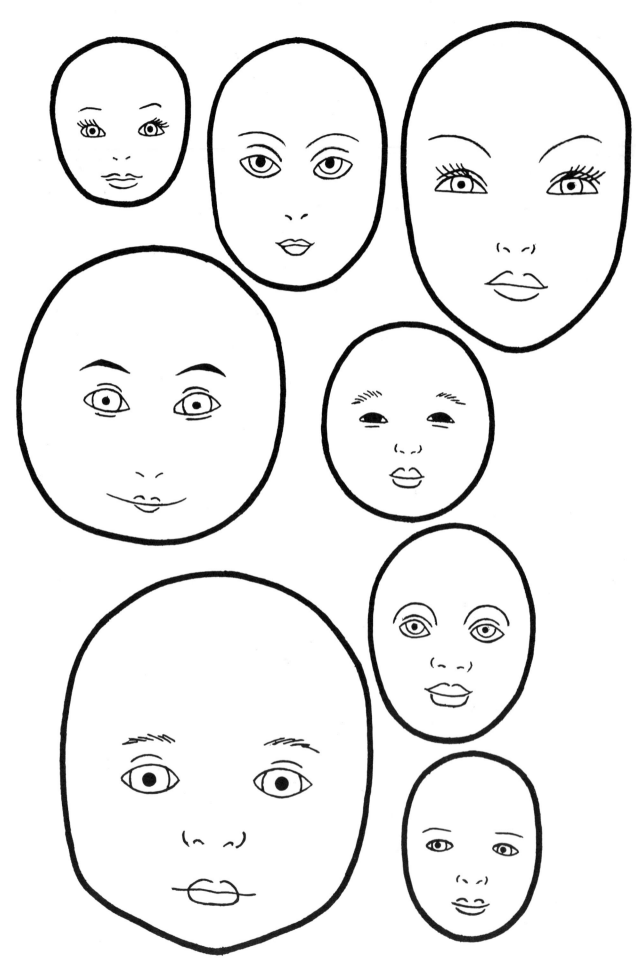

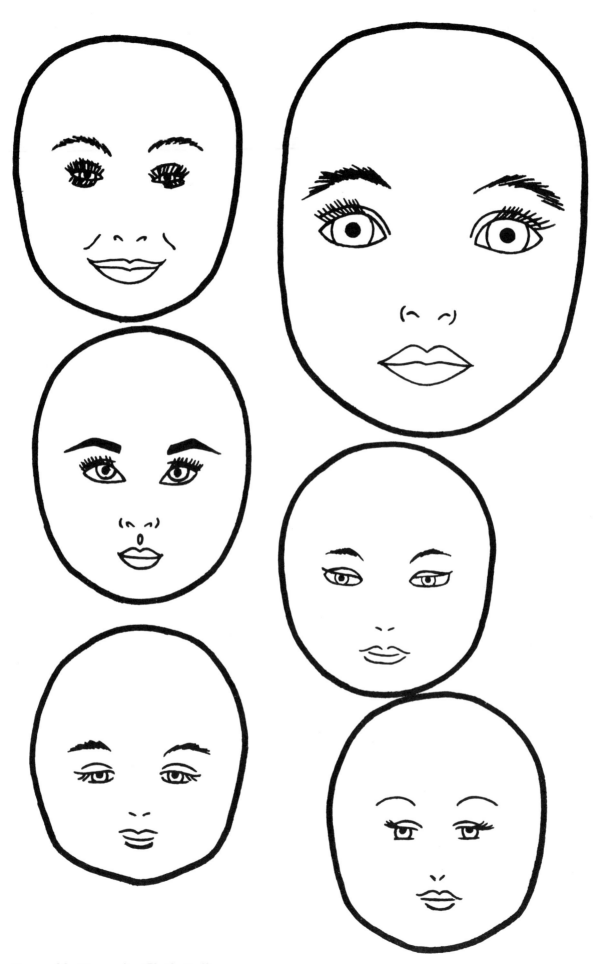

Make Your Hobby More Enjoyable With

THE MAGAZINE MADE FOR DOLLMAKERS

INSIDE EACH BI-MONTHLY ISSUE OF DOLLMAKING CRAFTS & DESIGNS YOU'LL FIND. . .

◆ DOLL PROJECTS FOR ALL SKILL LEVELS

◆ MORE PATTERNS

◆ PROBLEM SOLVING TIPS FOR CLOTH DOLLMAKERS

◆ PROJECTS FOR DRESSING & ACCESSORIZING DOLLS

◆ MORE NEW PRODUCTS & REVIEWS

◆ MORE ARTIST COLUMNS INCLUDING CLOTH DOLL & PATTERN DESIGNER, BARBARA SPENCER

◆ MUCH, MUCH MORE!

CREDIT CARD ORDERS CALL TODAY!
1-800-331-0038

Order Form

Traceable Faces for Cloth Dolls

☎ **Telephone Order:** Call 1-800-331-0038 and have your Mastercard, Visa, AMEX or Discover ready. Please mention code "10576."

✳ **Fax Orders:** Complete this form and fax it to 715-445-4053.

✉ **Mail Orders:** Mail this form, along with your check (unless paying by credit card), to: Jones Publishing
Book Orders, Dept. 10576
P.O. Box 5000
Iola, WI 54945

Address:

Company Name: _____

Name: _____

Address: _____

City: _____ State: _____ Zip: _____

Quantity	Title	Unit Price	Total
_____	*Traceable Faces for Cloth Dolls*	$ 9.95	$_____
_____	_____	$_____	$_____
_____	_____	$_____	$_____
		Subtotal	$_____

5.5% Sales Tax (Wisconsin residents only) .... $_____

*Shipping: $2.00 U.S., $5.00 Foreign .... $_____

TOTAL .... $_____

* If ordering more than one book, or a combination of this book and products from the advertisement on the previous page, refer to the shipping and handling chart in that advertisement.

Payment:

❏ Check (U.S. Funds)

❏ Visa   ❏ Mastercard   ❏ AMEX   ❏ Discover

Card Number: _____ Exp. Date: _____

Name on Card: _____

Signature: _____

Code: 10576